MW00960254

MY NAME

....

....

ISBN: 9781793916808
IMPRINT: INDEPENDENTLY PUBLISHED

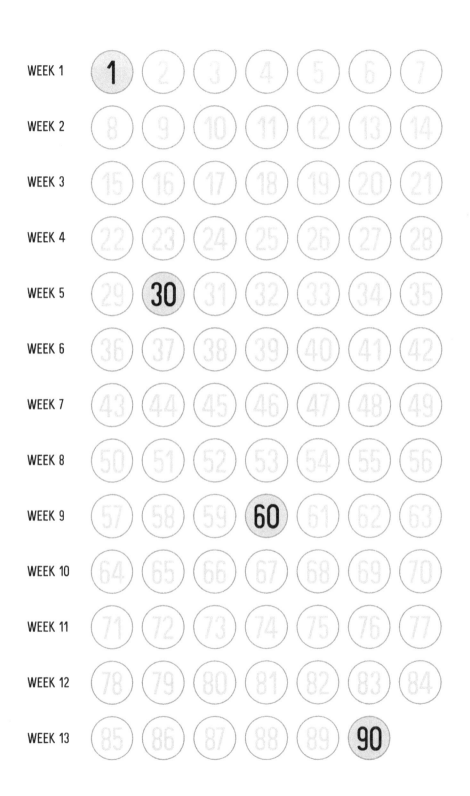

DAY ①

ARM ....

CHEST ....

WAIST ....

BELLY ....

HIP ....

THIGH ....

CALF ....

WEIGHT

....

BMI

....

MY GOALS ....
....
....
....
....

DAY (1)

MO TU WE TH FR SA SU

DATE ....

HOW I FEEL

BREAKFAST   LUNCH   DINNER

....
....
....
....
....

SNACKS

....
....
....
....

TOTAL CALORIES

_____ ___ ___

PROTEIN CONTENT FIBER CONTENT   WEIGHT   SLEEP   WATER   PROTEIN

_____ ___

OTHER

....

EXERCISE & ACTIVITY / MIND & SOUL   SET / REPS / DISTANCE   TIME

....
....
....
....
....

6A 7 8 9 10 11 12P 1 2 3 4 5 6 7 8 9 10+

B=BREAKFAST   L=LUNCH   D=DINNER   S=SNACKS   E=EXERCISE   M=MIND

HOW I FEEL

MO TU WE TH FR SA SU

DATE ....

DAY ②

BREAKFAST	LUNCH	DINNER

SNACKS

TOTAL CALORIES
_____

PROTEIN CONTENT FIBER CONTENT

WEIGHT   SLEEP   WATER   PROTEIN

OTHER
....

 EXERCISE & ACTIVITY / MIND & SOUL   SET / REPS / DISTANCE   TIME

6A 7 8 9 10 11 12P 1 2 3 4 5 6 7 8 9 10+

B=BREAKFAST   L=LUNCH   D=DINNER   S=SNACKS   E=EXERCISE   M=MIND

DAY ③

DATE ....

HOW I FEEL

😃 ◯ 🙂 ◯ 😐 ◯ ☹ ◯

BREAKFAST
....
....
....
....
....

SNACKS
....
....
....
....

LUNCH
....
....
....
....
....
....
....
....
....
....
....

DINNER
....
....
....
....
....
....
....
....
....
....
....

TOTAL CALORIES
_____

PROTEIN CONTENT   FIBER CONTENT
_____   _____

WEIGHT   SLEEP   WATER   PROTEIN

OTHER
....

♡ EXERCISE & ACTIVITY / MIND & SOUL   SET / REPS / DISTANCE   TIME
....
....
....
....
....

🕐 6A 7 8 9 10 11 12P 1 2 3 4 5 6 7 8 9 10+

B=BREAKFAST   L=LUNCH   D=DINNER   S=SNACKS   E=EXERCISE   M=MIND

HOW I FEEL

MO TU WE TH FR SA SU

DATE ....

DAY ④

BREAKFAST   LUNCH   DINNER

....
....
....
....
....
_____ ___ ___   ....

SNACKS   ....
....
....
....
....
_____ ___ ___   ....

TOTAL CALORIES

_____   WEIGHT   SLEEP   WATER   PROTEIN

PROTEIN CONTENT FIBER CONTENT

_____ ___ ___   _____   ....

OTHER

....

♡ EXERCISE & ACTIVITY / MIND & SOUL   SET / REPS / DISTANCE   TIME

....
....
....
....
....

🕐 6A 7 8 9 10 11 12P 1 2 3 4 5 6 7 8 9 10+

B=BREAKFAST   L=LUNCH   D=DINNER   S=SNACKS   E=EXERCISE   M=MIND

DAY (5)

MO TU WE TH FR SA SU

DATE ....

BREAKFAST ....LUNCH......................DINNER

....
....
....
....
....
_____ ____ ___

SNACKS
....
....
....
....

TOTAL CALORIES
_____

PROTEIN CONTENT FIBER CONTENT
_____ _____

OTHER
....

WEIGHT   SLEEP   WATER   PROTEIN

EXERCISE & ACTIVITY / MIND & SOUL   SET / REPS / DISTANCE   TIME

....
....
....
....
....

6A 7 8 9 10 11 12P 1 2 3 4 5 6 7 8 9 10+

B=BREAKFAST   L=LUNCH   D=DINNER   S=SNACKS   E=EXERCISE   M=MIND

HOW I FEEL

MO TU WE TH FR SA SU

DATE ....

DAY (6)

BREAKFAST   LUNCH   DINNER

....
....
....
....
....
___ ___ ___   ....

SNACKS   ....
....
....
....
....
___ ___ ___   ___ ___ ___   ___ ___ ___

TOTAL CALORIES

_____   WEIGHT   SLEEP   WATER   PROTEIN

PROTEIN CONTENT FIBER CONTENT

___ ___ ___   =====   ....

OTHER

....

EXERCISE & ACTIVITY / MIND & SOUL   SET / REPS / DISTANCE   TIME

....
....
....
....
_____   _____   _____

6A 7 8 9 10 11 12P 1 2 3 4 5 6 7 8 9 10+

B=BREAKFAST   L=LUNCH   D=DINNER   S=SNACKS   E=EXERCISE   M=MIND

DAY (7)

MO TU WE TH FR SA SU

DATE ....

HOW I FEEL

○   ○   ○   ○

BREAKFAST	LUNCH	DINNER

....

SNACKS

....

TOTAL CALORIES

_____

PROTEIN CONTENT FIBER CONTENT

_____ _____

OTHER

....

WEIGHT   SLEEP   WATER   PROTEIN

EXERCISE & ACTIVITY / MIND & SOUL	SET / REPS / DISTANCE	TIME

6A 7 8 9 10 11 12P 1 2 3 4 5 6 7 8 9 10+

B=BREAKFAST   L=LUNCH   D=DINNER   S=SNACKS   E=EXERCISE   M=MIND

HOW I FEEL

MO TU WE TH FR SA SU

DATE ....

DAY (8)

BREAKFAST

LUNCH

DINNER

SNACKS

TOTAL CALORIES
_____

PROTEIN CONTENT   FIBER CONTENT
_____   _____

OTHER
....

WEIGHT   SLEEP   WATER   PROTEIN

EXERCISE & ACTIVITY / MIND & SOUL   SET / REPS / DISTANCE   TIME

6A 7 8 9 10 11 12P 1 2 3 4 5 6 7 8 9 10+

B=BREAKFAST   L=LUNCH   D=DINNER   S=SNACKS   E=EXERCISE   M=MIND

DAY (9)

MO TU WE TH FR SA SU

DATE ....

😄 🙂 😐 🙁
○ ○ ○ ○

BREAKFAST	LUNCH	DINNER
....	....	....
....	....	....
....	....	....
....	....	....
....	....	....

___ ___ ___

SNACKS

....
....
....
....

___ ___ ___ ___ ___ ___

TOTAL CALORIES

_____

PROTEIN CONTENT FIBER CONTENT

_____ _____

WEIGHT   SLEEP   WATER   PROTEIN

OTHER

....

♥ EXERCISE & ACTIVITY / MIND & SOUL   SET / REPS / DISTANCE   TIME

.... | .... | ....
.... | .... | ....
.... | .... | ....
.... | .... | ....
.... | .... | ....

🕐 6A 7 8 9 10 11 12P 1 2 3 4 5 6 7 8 9 10+

B=BREAKFAST   L=LUNCH   D=DINNER   S=SNACKS   E=EXERCISE   M=MIND

HOW I FEEL

MO TU WE TH FR SA SU

DATE ....

DAY (10)

BREAKFAST

LUNCH

DINNER

SNACKS

TOTAL CALORIES

_____ ____ ____

PROTEIN CONTENT FIBER CONTENT

WEIGHT

SLEEP

WATER

PROTEIN

OTHER

EXERCISE & ACTIVITY / MIND & SOUL

SET / REPS / DISTANCE

TIME

6A 7 8 9 10 11 12P 1 2 3 4 5 6 7 8 9 10+

B=BREAKFAST   L=LUNCH   D=DINNER   S=SNACKS   E=EXERCISE   M=MIND

DAY (11)

MO TU WE TH FR SA SU

DATE ....

HOW I FEEL

BREAKFAST

LUNCH

DINNER

....
....
....
....
....
....

_____ ____ ___

SNACKS

....
....
....
....

TOTAL CALORIES

_____

PROTEIN CONTENT FIBER CONTENT

_____ _____

OTHER

....

WEIGHT

SLEEP

WATER

PROTEIN

EXERCISE & ACTIVITY / MIND & SOUL

SET / REPS / DISTANCE

TIME

6A 7 8 9 10 11 12P 1 2 3 4 5 6 7 8 9 10+

B=BREAKFAST   L=LUNCH   D=DINNER   S=SNACKS   E=EXERCISE   M=MIND

HOW I FEEL

MO TU WE TH FR SA SU

DATE ....

DAY (12)

BREAKFAST	LUNCH	DINNER

SNACKS

TOTAL CALORIES

PROTEIN CONTENT   FIBER CONTENT | WEIGHT | SLEEP | WATER | PROTEIN

OTHER

♡ EXERCISE & ACTIVITY / MIND & SOUL | SET / REPS / DISTANCE | TIME

🕐 6A 7 8 9 10 11 12P 1 2 3 4 5 6 7 8 9 10+

B=BREAKFAST   L=LUNCH   D=DINNER   S=SNACKS   E=EXERCISE   M=MIND

DAY (13)

MO TU WE TH FR SA SU

DATE ....

HOW I FEEL

😃 🙂 😐 🙁
○ ○ ○ ○

BREAKFAST

....
....
....
....
....

_____ ____ ____

SNACKS

....
....
....
....

_____ ____ ____

LUNCH

....
....
....
....
....
....
....
....
....
....
....

_____ ____ ____

DINNER

....
....
....
....
....
....
....
....
....
....
....

_____ ____

TOTAL CALORIES

_____

PROTEIN CONTENT   FIBER CONTENT

_____   _____

OTHER

....

WEIGHT   SLEEP   WATER   PROTEIN

_____   _____   ....

♡ EXERCISE & ACTIVITY / MIND & SOUL

SET / REPS / DISTANCE   TIME

....
....
....
....
....

🕐 6A 7 8 9 10 11 12P 1 2 3 4 5 6 7 8 9 10+

B=BREAKFAST   L=LUNCH   D=DINNER   S=SNACKS   E=EXERCISE   M=MIND

HOW I FEEL

MO TU WE TH FR SA SU

DATE ....

DAY (14)

BREAKFAST   LUNCH   DINNER

SNACKS

TOTAL CALORIES

WEIGHT   SLEEP   WATER   PROTEIN

PROTEIN CONTENT FIBER CONTENT

OTHER

EXERCISE & ACTIVITY / MIND & SOUL   SET / REPS / DISTANCE   TIME

6A 7 8 9 10 11 12P 1 2 3 4 5 6 7 8 9 10+

B=BREAKFAST   L=LUNCH   D=DINNER   S=SNACKS   E=EXERCISE   M=MIND

DAY (15)

DATE ....

HOW I FEEL

:D :) :| :(
O   O   O   O

BREAKFAST	LUNCH	DINNER
....	....	....
....	....	....
....	....	....
....	....	....
....	....	....

SNACKS

....
....
....
....

TOTAL CALORIES

_____

PROTEIN CONTENT   FIBER CONTENT

_____   _____

WEIGHT   SLEEP   WATER   PROTEIN

OTHER

....

EXERCISE & ACTIVITY / MIND & SOUL   SET / REPS / DISTANCE   TIME

....	....	....
....	....	....
....	....	....
....	....	....
....	....	....

6A 7 8 9 10 11 12P 1 2 3 4 5 6 7 8 9 10+

B=BREAKFAST   L=LUNCH   D=DINNER   S=SNACKS   E=EXERCISE   M=MIND

HOW I FEEL

MO TU WE TH FR SA SU

DATE ....

DAY (16)

BREAKFAST

LUNCH

DINNER

SNACKS

TOTAL CALORIES

PROTEIN CONTENT   FIBER CONTENT

WEIGHT   SLEEP   WATER   PROTEIN

OTHER

EXERCISE & ACTIVITY / MIND & SOUL   SET / REPS / DISTANCE   TIME

6A 7 8 9 10 11 12P 1 2 3 4 5 6 7 8 9 10+

B=BREAKFAST   L=LUNCH   D=DINNER   S=SNACKS   E=EXERCISE   M=MIND

DAY (17)

MO TU WE TH FR SA SU

DATE ....

BREAKFAST

....
....
....
....
....
....

———— ——— ——

SNACKS

....
....
....
....

TOTAL CALORIES

————————————————

PROTEIN CONTENT   FIBER CONTENT

——————————   ————————

OTHER

....

LUNCH

....
....
....
....
....
....
....
....
....
....
....

———— ——— ——— ————

DINNER

....
....
....
....
....
....
....
....
....
....
....

———————— ————————

WEIGHT   SLEEP   WATER   PROTEIN

======= ....

EXERCISE & ACTIVITY / MIND & SOUL   SET / REPS / DISTANCE   TIME

....
....
....
....
....

6A 7 8 9 10 11 12P 1 2 3 4 5 6 7 8 9 10+

B=BREAKFAST   L=LUNCH   D=DINNER   S=SNACKS   E=EXERCISE   M=MIND

HOW I FEEL

MO TU WE TH FR SA SU

DATE ....

DAY (18)

BREAKFAST

LUNCH

DINNER

SNACKS

TOTAL CALORIES

PROTEIN CONTENT   FIBER CONTENT

WEIGHT

SLEEP

WATER

PROTEIN

OTHER

EXERCISE & ACTIVITY / MIND & SOUL

SET / REPS / DISTANCE

TIME

6A 7 8 9 10 11 12P 1 2 3 4 5 6 7 8 9 10+

B=BREAKFAST   L=LUNCH   D=DINNER   S=SNACKS   E=EXERCISE   M=MIND

DAY (19)

MO TU WE TH FR SA SU

DATE ....

HOW I FEEL

BREAKFAST   LUNCH   DINNER

....
....
....
....
....

SNACKS

....
....
....
....

TOTAL CALORIES

_____

PROTEIN CONTENT   FIBER CONTENT   WEIGHT   SLEEP   WATER   PROTEIN

_____

OTHER

....

EXERCISE & ACTIVITY / MIND & SOUL   SET / REPS / DISTANCE   TIME

6A 7 8 9 10 11 12P 1 2 3 4 5 6 7 8 9 10+

B=BREAKFAST   L=LUNCH   D=DINNER   S=SNACKS   E=EXERCISE   M=MIND

HOW I FEEL

MO TU WE TH FR SA SU

DATE ....

DAY ⑳

BREAKFAST   LUNCH   DINNER

....
....
....
....
....
_____ ___ ___   ....

SNACKS   ....
....
....
....
....
_____ ___ ___   ___ ___ ___   ___ ___ ___

TOTAL CALORIES

_____   WEIGHT   SLEEP   WATER   PROTEIN

PROTEIN CONTENT FIBER CONTENT

_____ _____   =============   ....

OTHER
....

EXERCISE & ACTIVITY / MIND & SOUL   SET / REPS / DISTANCE   TIME

....
....
....
....
....
_____   _____   _____

 6A 7   8   9   10 11 12P 1   2   3   4   5   6   7   8   9   10+

B=BREAKFAST   L=LUNCH   D=DINNER   S=SNACKS   E=EXERCISE   M=MIND

DAY (21)

MO TU WE TH FR SA SU

DATE ....

BREAKFAST

....
....
....
....
....

SNACKS

....
....
....
....

LUNCH

DINNER

TOTAL CALORIES

_____

PROTEIN CONTENT   FIBER CONTENT

WEIGHT   SLEEP   WATER   PROTEIN

OTHER

....

EXERCISE & ACTIVITY / MIND & SOUL

SET / REPS / DISTANCE   TIME

6A 7 8 9 10 11 12P 1 2 3 4 5 6 7 8 9 10+

B=BREAKFAST   L=LUNCH   D=DINNER   S=SNACKS   E=EXERCISE   M=MIND

HOW I FEEL

MO TU WE TH FR SA SU

DATE ....

DAY (22)

BREAKFAST

....
....
....
....
....

SNACKS

....
....
....
....

LUNCH

....
....
....
....
....
....
....
....
....
....
....
....
....
....

DINNER

....
....
....
....
....
....
....
....
....
....
....
....
....

TOTAL CALORIES

_____

PROTEIN CONTENT   FIBER CONTENT

_____   _____

OTHER

....

WEIGHT   SLEEP   WATER   PROTEIN

EXERCISE & ACTIVITY / MIND & SOUL

SET / REPS / DISTANCE   TIME

....
....
....
....
....

6A 7 8 9 10 11 12P 1 2 3 4 5 6 7 8 9 10+

B=BREAKFAST   L=LUNCH   D=DINNER   S=SNACKS   E=EXERCISE   M=MIND

DAY (23)

MO TU WE TH FR SA SU

DATE ....

○   ○   ○   ○

BREAKFAST	LUNCH	DINNER
....	....	....
....	....	....
....	....	....
....	....	....
....	....	....

SNACKS

....

....

....

....

TOTAL CALORIES

_____

PROTEIN CONTENT   FIBER CONTENT

_____   _____

WEIGHT   SLEEP   WATER   PROTEIN

OTHER

....

♡ **EXERCISE & ACTIVITY / MIND & SOUL**   SET / REPS / DISTANCE   TIME

....	....	....
....	....	....
....	....	....
....	....	....

🕐   6A   7   8   9   10   11   12P   1   2   3   4   5   6   7   8   9   10+

B=BREAKFAST   L=LUNCH   D=DINNER   S=SNACKS   E=EXERCISE   M=MIND

HOW I FEEL

MO TU WE TH FR SA SU

DATE ....

DAY ㉔

BREAKFAST	LUNCH	DINNER
....	....	....
....	....	....
....	....	....
....	....	....
....	....	....

SNACKS

....

....

....

....

TOTAL CALORIES

_____ _____ _____

PROTEIN CONTENT FIBER CONTENT

_____ _____

OTHER

....

	WEIGHT	SLEEP	WATER	PROTEIN

 EXERCISE & ACTIVITY / MIND & SOUL   SET / REPS / DISTANCE   TIME

....	....	....
....	....	....
....	....	....
....	....	....
....	....	....

6A 7 8 9 10 11 12P 1 2 3 4 5 6 7 8 9 10+

B=BREAKFAST   L=LUNCH   D=DINNER   S=SNACKS   E=EXERCISE   M=MIND

DAY (25)

MO TU WE TH FR SA SU

DATE ....

HOW I FEEL

BREAKFAST
....
....
....
....
....
_____ _____ _____

SNACKS
....
....
....
....
....
_____ _____ _____

LUNCH

DINNER

TOTAL CALORIES
_____

PROTEIN CONTENT   FIBER CONTENT

WEIGHT   SLEEP   WATER   PROTEIN

OTHER
....

EXERCISE & ACTIVITY / MIND & SOUL   SET / REPS / DISTANCE   TIME

6A 7 8 9 10 11 12P 1 2 3 4 5 6 7 8 9 10+

B=BREAKFAST   L=LUNCH   D=DINNER   S=SNACKS   E=EXERCISE   M=MIND

HOW I FEEL

MO TU WE TH FR SA SU

DATE ....

DAY (26)

BREAKFAST | LUNCH | DINNER

SNACKS

TOTAL CALORIES

PROTEIN CONTENT FIBER CONTENT

WEIGHT | SLEEP | WATER | PROTEIN

OTHER

EXERCISE & ACTIVITY / MIND & SOUL | SET / REPS / DISTANCE | TIME

6A 7 8 9 10 11 12P 1 2 3 4 5 6 7 8 9 10+

B=BREAKFAST   L=LUNCH   D=DINNER   S=SNACKS   E=EXERCISE   M=MIND

DAY (27)

MO TU WE TH FR SA SU

DATE ....

○ ○ ○ ○

BREAKFAST	LUNCH	DINNER
....	....	....
....	....	....
....	....	....
....	....	....
....	....	....
—————— —— ——	....	....

SNACKS

....

....

....

....

—————— —— —— ....

—————— —— —— —————— —— ——

TOTAL CALORIES

————————————

WEIGHT   SLEEP   WATER   PROTEIN

PROTEIN CONTENT   FIBER CONTENT

———————   ————————   ————————   ....

OTHER

....

♥ EXERCISE & ACTIVITY / MIND & SOUL   SET / REPS / DISTANCE   TIME

....

....

....

....

....

——————————   ——————————   ——————————

🕐 6A 7 8 9 10 11 12P 1 2 3 4 5 6 7 8 9 10+

B=BREAKFAST   L=LUNCH   D=DINNER   S=SNACKS   E=EXERCISE   M=MIND

HOW I FEEL

MO TU WE TH FR SA SU

DATE ....

DAY ㉘

BREAKFAST

LUNCH

DINNER

SNACKS

TOTAL CALORIES

WEIGHT

SLEEP

WATER

PROTEIN

PROTEIN CONTENT   FIBER CONTENT

OTHER

EXERCISE & ACTIVITY / MIND & SOUL

SET / REPS / DISTANCE

TIME

6A 7 8 9 10 11 12P 1 2 3 4 5 6 7 8 9 10+

B=BREAKFAST   L=LUNCH   D=DINNER   S=SNACKS   E=EXERCISE   M=MIND

DAY (29)

MO TU WE TH FR SA SU

DATE ....

BREAKFAST

LUNCH

DINNER

SNACKS

TOTAL CALORIES

PROTEIN CONTENT   FIBER CONTENT

WEIGHT   SLEEP   WATER   PROTEIN

OTHER

♥ EXERCISE & ACTIVITY / MIND & SOUL   SET / REPS / DISTANCE   TIME

🕐 6A 7 8 9 10 11 12P 1 2 3 4 5 6 7 8 9 10+

B=BREAKFAST   L=LUNCH   D=DINNER   S=SNACKS   E=EXERCISE   M=MIND

DAY 30

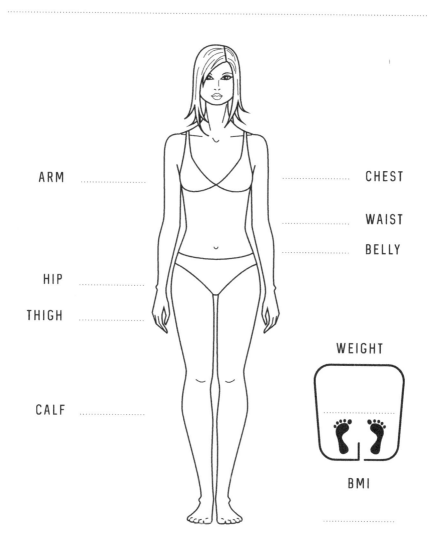

ARM ....

CHEST ....

WAIST ....

BELLY ....

HIP ....

THIGH ....

CALF ....

WEIGHT

BMI

NOTES

DAY (30)

DATE ....

HOW I FEEL

:D :) :| :(
O   O   O   O

BREAKFAST

LUNCH

DINNER

....
....
....
....
....

SNACKS

....
....
....
....

TOTAL CALORIES

_____

PROTEIN CONTENT   FIBER CONTENT

WEIGHT   SLEEP   WATER   PROTEIN

OTHER

....

♡ EXERCISE & ACTIVITY / MIND & SOUL   SET / REPS / DISTANCE   TIME

....
....
....
....
....

6A 7 8 9 10 11 12P 1 2 3 4 5 6 7 8 9 10+

B=BREAKFAST   L=LUNCH   D=DINNER   S=SNACKS   E=EXERCISE   M=MIND

HOW I FEEL

😀 🙂 😐 🙁
○ ○ ○ ○

MO TU WE TH FR SA SU

DATE ....

DAY (31)

BREAKFAST	LUNCH	DINNER
....		....
....		....
....		....
....		....
....		....
——— — —		

SNACKS

....
....
....
....

—— — ——   ——— — ——   ——— — ——

TOTAL CALORIES

_____

PROTEIN CONTENT   FIBER CONTENT

—— ——   —— ——

WEIGHT   SLEEP   WATER   PROTEIN

OTHER

....

EXERCISE & ACTIVITY / MIND & SOUL	SET / REPS / DISTANCE	TIME
....		....
....		....
....		....
....		....

6A 7 8 9 10 11 12P 1 2 3 4 5 6 7 8 9 10+

B=BREAKFAST   L=LUNCH   D=DINNER   S=SNACKS   E=EXERCISE   M=MIND

DAY (32)

DATE ....

HOW I FEEL

😄 🙂 😐 ☹
○ ○ ○ ○

BREAKFAST	LUNCH	DINNER

SNACKS

TOTAL CALORIES

WEIGHT   SLEEP   WATER   PROTEIN

PROTEIN CONTENT   FIBER CONTENT

OTHER

❤ EXERCISE & ACTIVITY / MIND & SOUL   SET / REPS / DISTANCE   TIME

🕐 6A 7 8 9 10 11 12P 1 2 3 4 5 6 7 8 9 10+

B=BREAKFAST   L=LUNCH   D=DINNER   S=SNACKS   E=EXERCISE   M=MIND

HOW I FEEL

MO TU WE TH FR SA SU

DATE ....

DAY (33)

BREAKFAST

....

....

....

....

....

_____ ____ ___

SNACKS

....

....

....

....

_____ ____ ___

TOTAL CALORIES

_____

PROTEIN CONTENT FIBER CONTENT

_____ ____

OTHER

....

LUNCH

....

....

....

....

....

....

....

....

....

....

....

....

WEIGHT

========

DINNER

....

....

....

....

....

....

....

....

....

....

....

SLEEP   WATER   PROTEIN

....

♥ EXERCISE & ACTIVITY / MIND & SOUL	SET / REPS / DISTANCE	TIME
....	....	....
....	....	....
....	....	....
....	....	....
....	....	....

🕐 6A 7 8 9 10 11 12P 1 2 3 4 5 6 7 8 9 10+

B=BREAKFAST   L=LUNCH   D=DINNER   S=SNACKS   E=EXERCISE   M=MIND

DAY (34)

DATE ....

HOW I FEEL

BREAKFAST   LUNCH   DINNER

....

SNACKS

TOTAL CALORIES

_____ ___ ___

PROTEIN CONTENT FIBER CONTENT

_____ ___ ___

OTHER

....

WEIGHT   SLEEP   WATER   PROTEIN

 EXERCISE & ACTIVITY / MIND & SOUL   SET / REPS / DISTANCE   TIME

6A 7 8 9 10 11 12P 1 2 3 4 5 6 7 8 9 10+

B=BREAKFAST   L=LUNCH   D=DINNER   S=SNACKS   E=EXERCISE   M=MIND

HOW I FEEL

MO TU WE TH FR SA SU

DATE ....

DAY (35)

BREAKFAST

LUNCH

DINNER

SNACKS

TOTAL CALORIES

WEIGHT　　SLEEP　　WATER　　PROTEIN

PROTEIN CONTENT FIBER CONTENT

OTHER

♥ EXERCISE & ACTIVITY / MIND & SOUL   SET / REPS / DISTANCE   TIME

🕐 6A 7 8 9 10 11 12P 1 2 3 4 5 6 7 8 9 10+

B=BREAKFAST   L=LUNCH   D=DINNER   S=SNACKS   E=EXERCISE   M=MIND

DAY (36)

MO TU WE TH FR SA SU

DATE ....

BREAKFAST
....
....
....
....
....
_____ ___ ___

SNACKS
....
....
....
....
_____ ___ ___

TOTAL CALORIES
_____

PROTEIN CONTENT   FIBER CONTENT
_____   _____

OTHER
....

LUNCH
....
....
....
....
....
....
....
....
....
....
....
....

DINNER
....
....
....
....
....
....
....
....
....
....
....

WEIGHT   SLEEP   WATER   PROTEIN

♥ **EXERCISE & ACTIVITY / MIND & SOUL**   SET / REPS / DISTANCE   TIME

....
....
....
....
....

🕐 6A 7 8 9 10 11 12P 1 2 3 4 5 6 7 8 9 10+

B=BREAKFAST   L=LUNCH   D=DINNER   S=SNACKS   E=EXERCISE   M=MIND

HOW I FEEL

MO TU WE TH FR SA SU

DATE ....

DAY (37)

BREAKFAST .... LUNCH .... DINNER

SNACKS

TOTAL CALORIES

WEIGHT   SLEEP   WATER   PROTEIN

PROTEIN CONTENT   FIBER CONTENT

OTHER

EXERCISE & ACTIVITY / MIND & SOUL   SET / REPS / DISTANCE   TIME

6A 7 8 9 10 11 12P 1 2 3 4 5 6 7 8 9 10+

B=BREAKFAST   L=LUNCH   D=DINNER   S=SNACKS   E=EXERCISE   M=MIND

DAY (38)

MO TU WE TH FR SA SU

DATE ....

BREAKFAST

....
....
....
....
....

SNACKS

....
....
....
....

LUNCH

....
....
....
....
....
....
....
....
....
....
....

DINNER

....
....
....
....
....
....
....
....
....
....
....

TOTAL CALORIES

_____

PROTEIN CONTENT   FIBER CONTENT

_____   _____

WEIGHT   SLEEP   WATER   PROTEIN

OTHER

....

♥ EXERCISE & ACTIVITY / MIND & SOUL   SET / REPS / DISTANCE   TIME

....
....
....
....
....

6A 7 8 9 10 11 12P 1 2 3 4 5 6 7 8 9 10+

B=BREAKFAST   L=LUNCH   D=DINNER   S=SNACKS   E=EXERCISE   M=MIND

HOW I FEEL

MO TU WE TH FR SA SU

DATE ....

DAY (39)

BREAKFAST

LUNCH

DINNER

SNACKS

TOTAL CALORIES

PROTEIN CONTENT   FIBER CONTENT

WEIGHT   SLEEP   WATER   PROTEIN

OTHER

EXERCISE & ACTIVITY / MIND & SOUL   SET / REPS / DISTANCE   TIME

6A 7   8   9   10 11 12P 1   2   3   4   5   6   7   8   9 10+

B=BREAKFAST   L=LUNCH   D=DINNER   S=SNACKS   E=EXERCISE   M=MIND

DAY (40)

MO TU WE TH FR SA SU

DATE ....

HOW I FEEL

😀 🙂 😐 ☹️
○ ○ ○ ○

BREAKFAST

LUNCH

DINNER

SNACKS

TOTAL CALORIES
_____

PROTEIN CONTENT FIBER CONTENT
_____ _____

WEIGHT   SLEEP   WATER   PROTEIN

OTHER
....

❤️ EXERCISE & ACTIVITY / MIND & SOUL   SET / REPS / DISTANCE   TIME

🕐 6A 7 8 9 10 11 12P 1 2 3 4 5 6 7 8 9 10+

B=BREAKFAST   L=LUNCH   D=DINNER   S=SNACKS   E=EXERCISE   M=MIND

HOW I FEEL

MO TU WE TH FR SA SU

DATE ....

DAY (41)

BREAKFAST

LUNCH

DINNER

....
....
....
....
....

SNACKS

....
....
....
....

TOTAL CALORIES

_____

PROTEIN CONTENT   FIBER CONTENT

WEIGHT   SLEEP   WATER   PROTEIN

OTHER

....

EXERCISE & ACTIVITY / MIND & SOUL   SET / REPS / DISTANCE   TIME

....
....
....
....

6A 7 8 9 10 11 12P 1 2 3 4 5 6 7 8 9 10+

B=BREAKFAST   L=LUNCH   D=DINNER   S=SNACKS   E=EXERCISE   M=MIND

DAY (42)

MO TU WE TH FR SA SU

DATE ....

○ ○ ○ ○

BREAKFAST

LUNCH

DINNER

....
....
....
....
....
....

____ ____ ____

SNACKS

....
....
....
....

____ ____ ____   ____ ____ ____

TOTAL CALORIES

_____

PROTEIN CONTENT FIBER CONTENT

WEIGHT   SLEEP   WATER   PROTEIN

_____ _____   ══════════ ....

OTHER

....

♡ EXERCISE & ACTIVITY / MIND & SOUL   SET / REPS / DISTANCE   TIME

....
....
....
....
....

6A 7 8 9 10 11 12P 1 2 3 4 5 6 7 8 9 10+

B=BREAKFAST   L=LUNCH   D=DINNER   S=SNACKS   E=EXERCISE   M=MIND

HOW I FEEL

MO TU WE TH FR SA SU

DATE ....

DAY (43)

BREAKFAST | LUNCH | DINNER

SNACKS

TOTAL CALORIES

PROTEIN CONTENT   FIBER CONTENT

WEIGHT   SLEEP   WATER   PROTEIN

OTHER
....

EXERCISE & ACTIVITY / MIND & SOUL   SET / REPS / DISTANCE   TIME

6A 7 8 9 10 11 12P 1 2 3 4 5 6 7 8 9 10+

B=BREAKFAST   L=LUNCH   D=DINNER   S=SNACKS   E=EXERCISE   M=MIND

DAY (44)

MO TU WE TH FR SA SU

DATE ....

HOW I FEEL

😄 ◯ 🙂 ◯ 😐 ◯ 🙁 ◯

BREAKFAST
....
....
....
....
....
....

SNACKS
....
....
....
....

TOTAL CALORIES
_____

PROTEIN CONTENT   FIBER CONTENT

LUNCH
....
....
....
....
....
....
....
....
....
....
....
....
....
....

DINNER
....
....
....
....
....
....
....
....
....
....

WEIGHT   SLEEP   WATER   PROTEIN

OTHER
....

❤ EXERCISE & ACTIVITY / MIND & SOUL

SET / REPS / DISTANCE   TIME

....
....
....
....
....

🕐 6A 7 8 9 10 11 12P 1 2 3 4 5 6 7 8 9 10+

B=BREAKFAST   L=LUNCH   D=DINNER   S=SNACKS   E=EXERCISE   M=MIND

HOW I FEEL

MO TU WE TH FR SA SU

DATE ....

DAY (45)

BREAKFAST | LUNCH | DINNER
.... | .... | ....
.... | .... | ....
.... | .... | ....
.... | .... | ....
.... | .... | ....
—— —— —— | .... | ....

SNACKS
.... | .... | ....
.... | .... | ....
.... | .... | ....
.... | .... | ....
—— —— —— | —— —— ——

TOTAL CALORIES

—————————————

WEIGHT | SLEEP | WATER | PROTEIN

PROTEIN CONTENT FIBER CONTENT

—————— —————— ═══════════ ....

OTHER
....

EXERCISE & ACTIVITY / MIND & SOUL   SET / REPS / DISTANCE   TIME
.... | .... | ....
.... | .... | ....
.... | .... | ....
.... | .... | ....

6A 7 8 9 10 11 12P 1 2 3 4 5 6 7 8 9 10+
B=BREAKFAST   L=LUNCH   D=DINNER   S=SNACKS   E=EXERCISE   M=MIND

DAY (46)

MO TU WE TH FR SA SU

DATE ....

HOW I FEEL

:D :) :| :(
O   O   O   O

BREAKFAST	LUNCH	DINNER

....
....
....
....
....

———— ——— ———

SNACKS

....
....
....
....

———— ——— ———

TOTAL CALORIES

————————————

WEIGHT   SLEEP   WATER   PROTEIN

PROTEIN CONTENT   FIBER CONTENT

———— ———

OTHER

....

♥ EXERCISE & ACTIVITY / MIND & SOUL	SET / REPS / DISTANCE	TIME

....
....
....
....
....

🕐 6A 7 8 9 10 11 12P 1 2 3 4 5 6 7 8 9 10+

B=BREAKFAST   L=LUNCH   D=DINNER   S=SNACKS   E=EXERCISE   M=MIND

HOW I FEEL

MO TU WE TH FR SA SU

DATE ....

DAY (47)

BREAKFAST

LUNCH

DINNER

....

....

....

....

....

SNACKS

....

....

....

....

TOTAL CALORIES

_____ ____ ____ ____

PROTEIN CONTENT FIBER CONTENT

WEIGHT

SLEEP

WATER

PROTEIN

OTHER

....

EXERCISE & ACTIVITY / MIND & SOUL

SET / REPS / DISTANCE

TIME

6A 7 8 9 10 11 12P 1 2 3 4 5 6 7 8 9 10+

B=BREAKFAST   L=LUNCH   D=DINNER   S=SNACKS   E=EXERCISE   M=MIND

DAY (48)

MO TU WE TH FR SA SU

DATE ....

HOW I FEEL

BREAKFAST   LUNCH   DINNER

....
....
....
....
....
___ ___ ___   ....

SNACKS   ....

....
....
....
....
___ ___ ___   ___ ___ ___   ___ ___ ___

TOTAL CALORIES

_____   WEIGHT   SLEEP   WATER   PROTEIN

PROTEIN CONTENT FIBER CONTENT

___ ___

OTHER

....

EXERCISE & ACTIVITY / MIND & SOUL   SET / REPS / DISTANCE   TIME

....
....
....
....
....

6A 7 8 9 10 11 12P 1 2 3 4 5 6 7 8 9 10+

B=BREAKFAST   L=LUNCH   D=DINNER   S=SNACKS   E=EXERCISE   M=MIND

HOW I FEEL

MO TU WE TH FR SA SU

DATE ....

DAY 49

BREAKFAST   LUNCH   DINNER

SNACKS

TOTAL CALORIES

PROTEIN CONTENT FIBER CONTENT   WEIGHT   SLEEP   WATER   PROTEIN

OTHER

EXERCISE & ACTIVITY / MIND & SOUL   SET / REPS / DISTANCE   TIME

6A 7 8 9 10 11 12P 1 2 3 4 5 6 7 8 9 10+

B=BREAKFAST   L=LUNCH   D=DINNER   S=SNACKS   E=EXERCISE   M=MIND

DAY (50)

MO TU WE TH FR SA SU

DATE ....

BREAKFAST

LUNCH

DINNER

....
....
....
....
....
....

SNACKS

....
....
....
....

TOTAL CALORIES

_____

PROTEIN CONTENT   FIBER CONTENT

WEIGHT   SLEEP   WATER   PROTEIN

_____ _____

OTHER

....

♥ EXERCISE & ACTIVITY / MIND & SOUL   SET / REPS / DISTANCE   TIME

🕐 6A 7 8 9 10 11 12P 1 2 3 4 5 6 7 8 9 10+

B=BREAKFAST   L=LUNCH   D=DINNER   S=SNACKS   E=EXERCISE   M=MIND

HOW I FEEL

MO TU WE TH FR SA SU

DATE ....

DAY 51

BREAKFAST

LUNCH

DINNER

SNACKS

TOTAL CALORIES

PROTEIN CONTENT   FIBER CONTENT

WEIGHT

SLEEP

WATER

PROTEIN

OTHER

EXERCISE & ACTIVITY / MIND & SOUL

SET / REPS / DISTANCE

TIME

6A 7 8 9 10 11 12P 1 2 3 4 5 6 7 8 9 10+

B=BREAKFAST   L=LUNCH   D=DINNER   S=SNACKS   E=EXERCISE   M=MIND

DAY (52)

MO TU WE TH FR SA SU

DATE ....

HOW I FEEL

☺ ☺ ☺ ☹
○ ○ ○ ○

BREAKFAST   LUNCH   DINNER

....
....
....
....
....
____ ___ ___

SNACKS

....
....
....
....
____ ___ ___

TOTAL CALORIES

_____   WEIGHT   SLEEP   WATER   PROTEIN

PROTEIN CONTENT FIBER CONTENT

____ ___   ======== ....

OTHER

....

♡ EXERCISE & ACTIVITY / MIND & SOUL   SET / REPS / DISTANCE   TIME

....
....
....
....
....

🕐 6A 7 8 9 10 11 12P 1 2 3 4 5 6 7 8 9 10+

B=BREAKFAST   L=LUNCH   D=DINNER   S=SNACKS   E=EXERCISE   M=MIND

HOW I FEEL

MO TU WE TH FR SA SU

DATE ....

DAY (53)

BREAKFAST

....
....
....
....
....
_____ _____ _____

SNACKS

....
....
....
....
_____ _____ _____

TOTAL CALORIES

_____

PROTEIN CONTENT   FIBER CONTENT

_____   _____

OTHER

....

LUNCH

....
....
....
....
....
....
....
....
....
....
....
....
....

DINNER

....
....
....
....
....
....
....
....
....
....
....
....
....

WEIGHT   SLEEP   WATER   PROTEIN

======   ....

EXERCISE & ACTIVITY / MIND & SOUL

SET / REPS / DISTANCE   TIME

....
....
....
....
....

6A 7 8 9 10 11 12P 1 2 3 4 5 6 7 8 9 10+

B=BREAKFAST   L=LUNCH   D=DINNER   S=SNACKS   E=EXERCISE   M=MIND

DAY (54)

MO TU WE TH FR SA SU

DATE ....

BREAKFAST
....
....
....
....
....

SNACKS
....
....
....
....

TOTAL CALORIES
_____

PROTEIN CONTENT   FIBER CONTENT
_____   _____

OTHER
....

LUNCH

DINNER

WEIGHT   SLEEP   WATER   PROTEIN

 EXERCISE & ACTIVITY / MIND & SOUL   SET / REPS / DISTANCE   TIME

6A 7 8 9 10 11 12P 1 2 3 4 5 6 7 8 9 10+

B=BREAKFAST   L=LUNCH   D=DINNER   S=SNACKS   E=EXERCISE   M=MIND

HOW I FEEL

MO TU WE TH FR SA SU

DATE ....

DAY (55)

BREAKFAST

LUNCH

DINNER

SNACKS

TOTAL CALORIES

_____

PROTEIN CONTENT FIBER CONTENT

WEIGHT

SLEEP

WATER

PROTEIN

OTHER

❤ EXERCISE & ACTIVITY / MIND & SOUL

SET / REPS / DISTANCE

TIME

🕐 6A 7 8 9 10 11 12P 1 2 3 4 5 6 7 8 9 10+

B=BREAKFAST   L=LUNCH   D=DINNER   S=SNACKS   E=EXERCISE   M=MIND

DAY (56)

DATE ....

HOW I FEEL

☺ ☺ ☺ ☹
○ ○ ○ ○

BREAKFAST

LUNCH

DINNER

SNACKS

TOTAL CALORIES

WEIGHT   SLEEP   WATER   PROTEIN

PROTEIN CONTENT FIBER CONTENT

OTHER

♡ EXERCISE & ACTIVITY / MIND & SOUL   SET / REPS / DISTANCE   TIME

🕐 6A 7 8 9 10 11 12P 1 2 3 4 5 6 7 8 9 10+

B=BREAKFAST   L=LUNCH   D=DINNER   S=SNACKS   E=EXERCISE   M=MIND

HOW I FEEL

MO TU WE TH FR SA SU

DATE ....

DAY (57)

BREAKFAST

LUNCH

DINNER

SNACKS

TOTAL CALORIES

PROTEIN CONTENT FIBER CONTENT

WEIGHT   SLEEP   WATER   PROTEIN

OTHER

EXERCISE & ACTIVITY / MIND & SOUL   SET / REPS / DISTANCE   TIME

6A 7 8 9 10 11 12P 1 2 3 4 5 6 7 8 9 10+

B=BREAKFAST   L=LUNCH   D=DINNER   S=SNACKS   E=EXERCISE   M=MIND

DAY (58)

MO TU WE TH FR SA SU

DATE ....

HOW I FEEL

:D :) :| :(

BREAKFAST

LUNCH

DINNER

....
....
....
....
....

——— ——— ———

SNACKS

....
....
....
....

——— ——— ———

TOTAL CALORIES

——————————————

PROTEIN CONTENT FIBER CONTENT

—————— ——————

OTHER

....

WEIGHT   SLEEP   WATER   PROTEIN

EXERCISE & ACTIVITY / MIND & SOUL   SET / REPS / DISTANCE   TIME

....
....
....
....
....

6A 7 8 9 10 11 12P 1 2 3 4 5 6 7 8 9 10+

B=BREAKFAST   L=LUNCH   D=DINNER   S=SNACKS   E=EXERCISE   M=MIND

HOW I FEEL

MO TU WE TH FR SA SU

DATE ....

DAY (59)

BREAKFAST   LUNCH   DINNER

....

....

....

....

....

_____ _____ _____   ....

SNACKS

....

....

....

....

_____ _____ _____   _____ _____   _____ _____

TOTAL CALORIES

_____   WEIGHT   SLEEP   WATER   PROTEIN

PROTEIN CONTENT FIBER CONTENT

_____   _____

OTHER

....

EXERCISE & ACTIVITY / MIND & SOUL   SET / REPS / DISTANCE   TIME

....

....

....

....

_____   _____   _____

6A 7   8   9   10 11 12P 1   2   3   4   5   6   7   8   9 10+

B=BREAKFAST   L=LUNCH   D=DINNER   S=SNACKS   E=EXERCISE   M=MIND

DAY 60

ARM ....

CHEST ....

WAIST ....

BELLY ....

HIP ....

THIGH ....

CALF ....

WEIGHT

BMI

....

NOTES
....
....
....
....
....

HOW I FEEL

MO TU WE TH FR SA SU

DATE ....

DAY (60)

BREAKFAST   LUNCH   DINNER

SNACKS

TOTAL CALORIES

PROTEIN CONTENT   FIBER CONTENT   WEIGHT   SLEEP   WATER   PROTEIN

OTHER

EXERCISE & ACTIVITY / MIND & SOUL   SET / REPS / DISTANCE   TIME

6A 7 8 9 10 11 12P 1 2 3 4 5 6 7 8 9 10+

B=BREAKFAST   L=LUNCH   D=DINNER   S=SNACKS   E=EXERCISE   M=MIND

DAY (61)

DATE ....

HOW I FEEL

☺   ☺   😐   ☹
○   ○   ○   ○

BREAKFAST

LUNCH

DINNER

....
....
....
....
....

SNACKS

....
....
....
....

TOTAL CALORIES

_____

PROTEIN CONTENT   FIBER CONTENT

_____   _____

OTHER

....

WEIGHT   SLEEP   WATER   PROTEIN

♡ EXERCISE & ACTIVITY / MIND & SOUL   SET / REPS / DISTANCE   TIME

....
....
....
....
....

🕐 6A 7 8 9 10 11 12P 1 2 3 4 5 6 7 8 9 10+

B=BREAKFAST   L=LUNCH   D=DINNER   S=SNACKS   E=EXERCISE   M=MIND

HOW I FEEL

MO TU WE TH FR SA SU

DATE ....

DAY (62)

BREAKFAST
....
....
....
....
....

SNACKS
....
....
....
....

TOTAL CALORIES
_____

PROTEIN CONTENT FIBER CONTENT

_____ _____

OTHER
....

LUNCH
....
....
....
....
....
....
....
....
....
....
....
....

DINNER
....
....
....
....
....
....

WEIGHT   SLEEP   WATER   PROTEIN

_____ _____ ....

EXERCISE & ACTIVITY / MIND & SOUL   SET / REPS / DISTANCE   TIME
....
....
....
....
....

6A 7 8 9 10 11 12P 1 2 3 4 5 6 7 8 9 10+

B=BREAKFAST   L=LUNCH   D=DINNER   S=SNACKS   E=EXERCISE   M=MIND

DAY (63)

HOW I FEEL

BREAKFAST

LUNCH

DINNER

....
....
....
....
....

SNACKS

....
....
....
....

TOTAL CALORIES
_____

PROTEIN CONTENT   FIBER CONTENT
_____   _____

OTHER
....

WEIGHT   SLEEP   WATER   PROTEIN

 EXERCISE & ACTIVITY / MIND & SOUL   SET / REPS / DISTANCE   TIME

....
....
....
....
....

6A 7 8 9 10 11 12P 1 2 3 4 5 6 7 8 9 10+

B=BREAKFAST   L=LUNCH   D=DINNER   S=SNACKS   E=EXERCISE   M=MIND

HOW I FEEL

MO TU WE TH FR SA SU

DATE ....

DAY (64)

BREAKFAST

LUNCH

DINNER

SNACKS

TOTAL CALORIES

PROTEIN CONTENT   FIBER CONTENT

WEIGHT

SLEEP

WATER

PROTEIN

OTHER

EXERCISE & ACTIVITY / MIND & SOUL

SET / REPS / DISTANCE   TIME

6A 7   8   9   10 11 12P 1   2   3   4   5   6   7   8   9 10+

B=BREAKFAST   L=LUNCH   D=DINNER   S=SNACKS   E=EXERCISE   M=MIND

DAY (65)

MO TU WE TH FR SA SU

DATE ....

HOW I FEEL

BREAKFAST   LUNCH   DINNER

....
....
....
....
....

SNACKS   ....

....
....
....
....

TOTAL CALORIES

─────────────   WEIGHT   SLEEP   WATER   PROTEIN

PROTEIN CONTENT FIBER CONTENT

OTHER
....

♡ EXERCISE & ACTIVITY / MIND & SOUL   SET / REPS / DISTANCE   TIME

....
....
....
....
....

🕐 6A 7 8 9 10 11 12P 1 2 3 4 5 6 7 8 9 10+

B=BREAKFAST   L=LUNCH   D=DINNER   S=SNACKS   E=EXERCISE   M=MIND

HOW I FEEL

MO TU WE TH FR SA SU

DATE ....

DAY (66)

BREAKFAST

LUNCH

DINNER

SNACKS

TOTAL CALORIES

_____

PROTEIN CONTENT   FIBER CONTENT

WEIGHT

SLEEP

WATER

PROTEIN

OTHER

♡ EXERCISE & ACTIVITY / MIND & SOUL

SET / REPS / DISTANCE

TIME

6A 7 8 9 10 11 12P 1 2 3 4 5 6 7 8 9 10+

B=BREAKFAST   L=LUNCH   D=DINNER   S=SNACKS   E=EXERCISE   M=MIND

DAY (67)

DATE

MO TU WE TH FR SA SU

BREAKFAST

LUNCH

DINNER

SNACKS

TOTAL CALORIES

PROTEIN CONTENT   FIBER CONTENT

WEIGHT   SLEEP   WATER   PROTEIN

OTHER

EXERCISE & ACTIVITY / MIND & SOUL

SET / REPS / DISTANCE   TIME

6A 7 8 9 10 11 12P 1 2 3 4 5 6 7 8 9 10+

B=BREAKFAST   L=LUNCH   D=DINNER   S=SNACKS   E=EXERCISE   M=MIND

HOW I FEEL

MO TU WE TH FR SA SU

DATE ....

DAY (68)

BREAKFAST	LUNCH	DINNER

SNACKS

TOTAL CALORIES

WEIGHT   SLEEP   WATER   PROTEIN

PROTEIN CONTENT   FIBER CONTENT

OTHER

♥ EXERCISE & ACTIVITY / MIND & SOUL

SET / REPS / DISTANCE   TIME

🕐 6A 7 8 9 10 11 12P 1 2 3 4 5 6 7 8 9 10+

B=BREAKFAST   L=LUNCH   D=DINNER   S=SNACKS   E=EXERCISE   M=MIND

DAY (69)

MO TU WE TH FR SA SU

DATE ....

HOW I FEEL

☺ ☺ ☺ ☹
○ ○ ○ ○

BREAKFAST
....
....
....
....
....
——— ——— ———

SNACKS
....
....
....
....
——— ——— ———

TOTAL CALORIES
————————————————

PROTEIN CONTENT FIBER CONTENT
———————— ————————

OTHER
....

LUNCH
....
....
....
....
....
....
....
....
....
....

DINNER
....
....
....
....
....
....
....
....
....
....

WEIGHT   SLEEP   WATER   PROTEIN
======== ....

♥ EXERCISE & ACTIVITY / MIND & SOUL   SET / REPS / DISTANCE   TIME
....
....
....
....
....

🕐 6A 7 8 9 10 11 12P 1 2 3 4 5 6 7 8 9 10+

B=BREAKFAST   L=LUNCH   D=DINNER   S=SNACKS   E=EXERCISE   M=MIND

HOW I FEEL

MO TU WE TH FR SA SU

DATE ....

DAY 70

BREAKFAST

LUNCH

DINNER

SNACKS

TOTAL CALORIES

PROTEIN CONTENT FIBER CONTENT

WEIGHT

SLEEP

WATER

PROTEIN

OTHER

EXERCISE & ACTIVITY / MIND & SOUL

SET / REPS / DISTANCE

TIME

6A 7 8 9 10 11 12P 1 2 3 4 5 6 7 8 9 10+

B=BREAKFAST   L=LUNCH   D=DINNER   S=SNACKS   E=EXERCISE   M=MIND

DAY (71)

MO TU WE TH FR SA SU

DATE ....

HOW I FEEL

BREAKFAST

LUNCH

DINNER

SNACKS

TOTAL CALORIES

_____

PROTEIN CONTENT FIBER CONTENT

_____ _____

OTHER

WEIGHT   SLEEP   WATER   PROTEIN

♡ EXERCISE & ACTIVITY / MIND & SOUL   SET / REPS / DISTANCE   TIME

🕐 6A 7 8 9 10 11 12P 1 2 3 4 5 6 7 8 9 10+

B=BREAKFAST   L=LUNCH   D=DINNER   S=SNACKS   E=EXERCISE   M=MIND

HOW I FEEL

MO TU WE TH FR SA SU

DATE ....

DAY (72)

BREAKFAST

....

....

....

....

....

.... ____   ____   ____

SNACKS

....

....

....

....

TOTAL CALORIES

_____

PROTEIN CONTENT   FIBER CONTENT

____   ____   ____

OTHER

....

....

LUNCH

DINNER

WEIGHT   SLEEP   WATER   PROTEIN

♡ EXERCISE & ACTIVITY / MIND & SOUL

SET / REPS / DISTANCE   TIME

6A 7 8 9 10 11 12P 1 2 3 4 5 6 7 8 9 10+

B=BREAKFAST   L=LUNCH   D=DINNER   S=SNACKS   E=EXERCISE   M=MIND

DAY (73)

MO TU WE TH FR SA SU

DATE ....

BREAKFAST

LUNCH

DINNER

....

....

....

....

....

SNACKS

....

....

....

....

TOTAL CALORIES

PROTEIN CONTENT FIBER CONTENT

WEIGHT   SLEEP   WATER   PROTEIN

OTHER

....

EXERCISE & ACTIVITY / MIND & SOUL   SET / REPS / DISTANCE   TIME

....

....

....

....

6A 7 8 9 10 11 12P 1 2 3 4 5 6 7 8 9 10+

B=BREAKFAST   L=LUNCH   D=DINNER   S=SNACKS   E=EXERCISE   M=MIND

HOW I FEEL

MO TU WE TH FR SA SU

DATE ....

DAY (74)

BREAKFAST

LUNCH

DINNER

SNACKS

TOTAL CALORIES

PROTEIN CONTENT FIBER CONTENT

WEIGHT

SLEEP

WATER

PROTEIN

OTHER

♡ EXERCISE & ACTIVITY / MIND & SOUL

SET / REPS / DISTANCE

TIME

6A 7 8 9 10 11 12P 1 2 3 4 5 6 7 8 9 10+

B=BREAKFAST L=LUNCH D=DINNER S=SNACKS E=EXERCISE M=MIND

DAY (75)

MO TU WE TH FR SA SU

DATE ....

HOW I FEEL

☺ ☺ ☺ ☹
○ ○ ○ ○

BREAKFAST

LUNCH

DINNER

....

SNACKS

TOTAL CALORIES

WEIGHT SLEEP WATER PROTEIN

PROTEIN CONTENT FIBER CONTENT

OTHER

❤ EXERCISE & ACTIVITY / MIND & SOUL

SET / REPS / DISTANCE   TIME

🕐 6A 7 8 9 10 11 12P 1 2 3 4 5 6 7 8 9 10+

B=BREAKFAST   L=LUNCH   D=DINNER   S=SNACKS   E=EXERCISE   M=MIND

HOW I FEEL

MO TU WE TH FR SA SU

DATE ....

DAY (76)

BREAKFAST   LUNCH   DINNER

SNACKS

TOTAL CALORIES

PROTEIN CONTENT   FIBER CONTENT   WEIGHT   SLEEP   WATER   PROTEIN

OTHER

EXERCISE & ACTIVITY / MIND & SOUL   SET / REPS / DISTANCE   TIME

6A   7   8   9   10   11   12P   1   2   3   4   5   6   7   8   9   10+
B=BREAKFAST   L=LUNCH   D=DINNER   S=SNACKS   E=EXERCISE   M=MIND

DAY (77)

MO TU WE TH FR SA SU

DATE ....

BREAKFAST
....
....
....
....
....

LUNCH

DINNER
....
....
....
....
....

SNACKS
....
....
....
....

TOTAL CALORIES
_____

PROTEIN CONTENT   FIBER CONTENT
_____   ____   ____

WEIGHT   SLEEP   WATER   PROTEIN

OTHER
....

EXERCISE & ACTIVITY / MIND & SOUL   SET / REPS / DISTANCE   TIME

6A 7 8 9 10 11 12P 1 2 3 4 5 6 7 8 9 10+

B=BREAKFAST   L=LUNCH   D=DINNER   S=SNACKS   E=EXERCISE   M=MIND

HOW I FEEL

MO TU WE TH FR SA SU

DATE ....

DAY (78)

BREAKFAST   LUNCH   DINNER

SNACKS

TOTAL CALORIES

WEIGHT   SLEEP   WATER   PROTEIN

PROTEIN CONTENT FIBER CONTENT

OTHER

EXERCISE & ACTIVITY / MIND & SOUL   SET / REPS / DISTANCE   TIME

6A 7 8 9 10 11 12P 1 2 3 4 5 6 7 8 9 10+

B=BREAKFAST   L=LUNCH   D=DINNER   S=SNACKS   E=EXERCISE   M=MIND

DAY (79)

MO TU WE TH FR SA SU

DATE ....

HOW I FEEL

😀 ○ 🙂 ○ 😐 ○ 🙁 ○

BREAKFAST

....
....
....
....
....

SNACKS

....
....
....
....

TOTAL CALORIES

_____

PROTEIN CONTENT FIBER CONTENT

_____ _____

OTHER

....

LUNCH

....
....
....
....
....
....
....
....
....
....
....

DINNER

....
....
....
....
....
....
....
....
....
....
....

WEIGHT   SLEEP   WATER   PROTEIN

....

♡/\/ EXERCISE & ACTIVITY / MIND & SOUL   SET / REPS / DISTANCE   TIME

....
....
....
....

🕐 6A 7 8 9 10 11 12P 1 2 3 4 5 6 7 8 9 10+

B = BREAKFAST   L = LUNCH   D = DINNER   S = SNACKS   E = EXERCISE   M = MIND

HOW I FEEL

MO TU WE TH FR SA SU

DATE ....

DAY (80)

BREAKFAST

....
....
....
....
....

SNACKS

....
....
....
....

TOTAL CALORIES

_____

PROTEIN CONTENT   FIBER CONTENT

_____   _____

OTHER

....

LUNCH

....
....
....
....
....
....
....
....
....
....
....

DINNER

....
....
....
....
....
....
....
....
....

WEIGHT   SLEEP   WATER   PROTEIN

♡ EXERCISE & ACTIVITY / MIND & SOUL   SET / REPS / DISTANCE   TIME

....
....
....
....

6A 7 8 9 10 11 12P 1 2 3 4 5 6 7 8 9 10+

B=BREAKFAST   L=LUNCH   D=DINNER   S=SNACKS   E=EXERCISE   M=MIND

DAY (81)

MO TU WE TH FR SA SU

DATE ....

HOW I FEEL

BREAKFAST

LUNCH

DINNER

SNACKS

TOTAL CALORIES

PROTEIN CONTENT FIBER CONTENT

WEIGHT   SLEEP   WATER   PROTEIN

OTHER

EXERCISE & ACTIVITY / MIND & SOUL   SET / REPS / DISTANCE   TIME

6A   7   8   9   10   11   12P   1   2   3   4   5   6   7   8   9   10+

B=BREAKFAST   L=LUNCH   D=DINNER   S=SNACKS   E=EXERCISE   M=MIND

HOW I FEEL

MO TU WE TH FR SA SU

DATE ....

DAY (82)

BREAKFAST	LUNCH	DINNER
....	....	....
....	....	....
....	....	....
....	....	....
....	....	....

SNACKS

....

....

....

....

TOTAL CALORIES

_____

PROTEIN CONTENT   FIBER CONTENT

WEIGHT   SLEEP   WATER   PROTEIN

OTHER

....

♥ EXERCISE & ACTIVITY / MIND & SOUL   SET / REPS / DISTANCE   TIME

....	....	....
....	....	....
....	....	....
....	....	....

6A 7 8 9 10 11 12P 1 2 3 4 5 6 7 8 9 10+

B=BREAKFAST   L=LUNCH   D=DINNER   S=SNACKS   E=EXERCISE   M=MIND

DAY (83)

MO TU WE TH FR SA SU

DATE ....

BREAKFAST

LUNCH

DINNER

SNACKS

TOTAL CALORIES

PROTEIN CONTENT   FIBER CONTENT

WEIGHT   SLEEP   WATER   PROTEIN

OTHER

 EXERCISE & ACTIVITY / MIND & SOUL   SET / REPS / DISTANCE   TIME

6A 7   8   9   10 11 12P 1   2   3   4   5   6   7   8   9 10+

B=BREAKFAST   L=LUNCH   D=DINNER   S=SNACKS   E=EXERCISE   M=MIND

HOW I FEEL

MO TU WE TH FR SA SU

DATE ....

DAY (84)

BREAKFAST   LUNCH   DINNER

....
....
....
....
....

SNACKS

....
....
....
....

TOTAL CALORIES

_____ __ __ ___   WEIGHT   SLEEP   WATER   PROTEIN

PROTEIN CONTENT FIBER CONTENT

_____ __ __ ___   ===========   ....

OTHER

....

EXERCISE & ACTIVITY / MIND & SOUL   SET / REPS / DISTANCE   TIME

....
....
....
....

6A 7   8   9   10 11 12P 1   2   3   4   5   6   7   8   9   10+

B=BREAKFAST   L=LUNCH   D=DINNER   S=SNACKS   E=EXERCISE   M=MIND

DAY (85)

DATE ....

HOW I FEEL

BREAKFAST

LUNCH

DINNER

SNACKS

TOTAL CALORIES

WEIGHT   SLEEP   WATER   PROTEIN

PROTEIN CONTENT   FIBER CONTENT

OTHER

EXERCISE & ACTIVITY / MIND & SOUL   SET / REPS / DISTANCE   TIME

6A 7 8 9 10 11 12P 1 2 3 4 5 6 7 8 9 10+

B=BREAKFAST   L=LUNCH   D=DINNER   S=SNACKS   E=EXERCISE   M=MIND

HOW I FEEL

MO TU WE TH FR SA SU

DATE ....

DAY (86)

BREAKFAST

LUNCH

DINNER

SNACKS

TOTAL CALORIES

PROTEIN CONTENT   FIBER CONTENT

WEIGHT

SLEEP

WATER

PROTEIN

OTHER

EXERCISE & ACTIVITY / MIND & SOUL   SET / REPS / DISTANCE   TIME

6A   7   8   9   10   11   12P   1   2   3   4   5   6   7   8   9   10+

B=BREAKFAST   L=LUNCH   D=DINNER   S=SNACKS   E=EXERCISE   M=MIND

DAY (87)

MO TU WE TH FR SA SU

DATE ....

HOW I FEEL

BREAKFAST

LUNCH

DINNER

SNACKS

TOTAL CALORIES

_____

PROTEIN CONTENT   FIBER CONTENT

_____   _____

OTHER

WEIGHT   SLEEP   WATER   PROTEIN

♥ EXERCISE & ACTIVITY / MIND & SOUL   SET / REPS / DISTANCE   TIME

🕐 6A 7 8 9 10 11 12P 1 2 3 4 5 6 7 8 9 10+

B=BREAKFAST   L=LUNCH   D=DINNER   S=SNACKS   E=EXERCISE   M=MIND

HOW I FEEL

MO TU WE TH FR SA SU

DATE ....

DAY (88)

BREAKFAST .... LUNCH .... DINNER

SNACKS

TOTAL CALORIES
_____

PROTEIN CONTENT   FIBER CONTENT   WEIGHT   SLEEP   WATER   PROTEIN

OTHER

EXERCISE & ACTIVITY / MIND & SOUL   SET / REPS / DISTANCE   TIME

6A 7 8 9 10 11 12P 1 2 3 4 5 6 7 8 9 10+

B=BREAKFAST   L=LUNCH   D=DINNER   S=SNACKS   E=EXERCISE   M=MIND

DAY (89)

MO TU WE TH FR SA SU

DATE ....

HOW I FEEL

:D :) :| :(
O   O   O   O

BREAKFAST

LUNCH

DINNER

....

....

....

....

....

SNACKS

....

....

....

....

TOTAL CALORIES

_____ ____ ____

PROTEIN CONTENT FIBER CONTENT

WEIGHT   SLEEP   WATER   PROTEIN

_____ _____   ========== ....

OTHER

....

♡ EXERCISE & ACTIVITY / MIND & SOUL   SET / REPS / DISTANCE   TIME

....

....

....

....

....

🕐 6A 7 8 9 10 11 12P 1 2 3 4 5 6 7 8 9 10+

B=BREAKFAST   L=LUNCH   D=DINNER   S=SNACKS   E=EXERCISE   M=MIND

HOW I FEEL

MO TU WE TH FR SA SU

DATE ....

DAY (90)

BREAKFAST	LUNCH	DINNER
....	....	....
....	....	....
....	....	....
....	....	....
....	....	....

SNACKS

....

....

....

....

_____ ____ ____

TOTAL CALORIES

_____

PROTEIN CONTENT   FIBER CONTENT

WEIGHT   SLEEP   WATER   PROTEIN

_____ ____   _____   ....

OTHER

....

♡ EXERCISE & ACTIVITY / MIND & SOUL   SET / REPS / DISTANCE   TIME

....	....	....
....	....	....
....	....	....
....	....	....
....	....	....

🕐 6A 7 8 9 10 11 12P 1 2 3 4 5 6 7 8 9 10+

B=BREAKFAST   L=LUNCH   D=DINNER   S=SNACKS   E=EXERCISE   M=MIND

DAY 90

ARM ....

HIP ....

THIGH ....

CALF ....

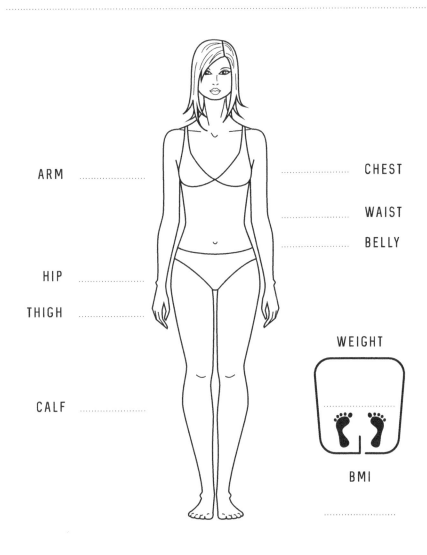

CHEST ....

WAIST ....

BELLY ....

WEIGHT

BMI

NOTES ....
....
....
....
....

MY RESULTS

DAY **1**

DAY **90**

DIFFERENCE

ARM

CHEST

WAIST

BELLY

HIP

THIGH

CALF

WEIGHT

WEIGHT

WEIGHT

BMI

BMI

BMI

NOTES

COPYRIGHT © STUDIO 5519
PUBLISHED BY: STUDIO 5519, 1732 1ST AVE #25519 NEW YORK, NY 10128
JANUARY 2019, ISSUE NO. 1 [V 1.0]: CONTACT: INFO@STUDIO5519.COM;
ILLUSTRATION CREDITS: © DEPOSITPHOTOS / @ PUSHINKA11 / @ GLEB_GURALNYK

Made in the USA
Las Vegas, NV
14 August 2024

93847343R00059